Fathers Matter

Leadership Lessons I've learned From

My Father

Cherie,

Thank you for supporting my dream. Continue doing your inner work. Spread Love

Jesse Ross

DEDICATION

This book is dedicated first to my father. Who inspired me to write this book. Far from perfect, but tried your hardest to do the best with what you had. I appreciate you for stepping up after my mother died. I can never repay you for what you've done for me. But, I can show my gratitude by what I pour into my kids, my family, and my community. Thank you for being an example. Forever indebted to you. Let's go to New York City!

SELF-PUBLISHING
SCHOOL

NOW IT'S YOUR TURN

Discover the EXACT 3-step blueprint you need to become a bestselling author in 3 months.

Self-Publishing School helped me, and now I want them to help you with this FREE WEBINAR!

Even if you're busy, bad at writing, or don't know where to start, you CAN write a bestseller and build your best life.

With tools and experience across a variety niches and professions, Self-Publishing School is the <u>only</u> resource you need to take your book to the finish line!

DON'T WAIT

Watch this FREE WEBINAR now, and
Say "YES" to becoming a bestseller:

[AFFILIATE LINK BELOW]
https://xe172.isrefer.com/go/sps4fta-vts/jesseross03

CONTENTS

Acknowledgements

To my mother, Shelby Berry. You are forever loved and missed.

To my family, everything I do is for you.

To my community, I believe in you.

To every person who reads this book, thank you for your support.

Introduction

This book is a dedication to one of the most difficult but favorite men in my life. My father and I are very similar in some ways. He's a strong, compassionate, stubborn, and helpful man. He tries his best to look out for people and to do everything with a spirit of excellence. I often tell people that when I grew up, he was in and out of my life. Meaning, he was there as much as he knew how to, or as much as my mother allowed him to. He was navigating a lot of moving parts in his life with work and social life. My father was as present as he knew how to be. But when he was present, we had the best of times. My mother passed away when I was eleven years old and my grandmother (her mother) wanted me to move down to Mississippi where she was. My dad stepped in and said that he was not going to allow that to happen. I don't think I've ever told him, but I'm so thankful that he did not let me move to Mississippi. That time in my life was one of the most difficult but life changing times in my life. When I made the transition from living with just my mother and I, to moving in with my father, my uncle, my little brother (nine years younger), and my older cousin, I struggled. The adjustment was huge. Not to mention, at eleven years old, you don't really know how to process death well.

My father and I bumped heads a lot. We had some disagreements, and I started to resent him for not letting me go live with my grandmother. I started to feel like I was a charity case and honestly felt my father only took me in because he could get some money from my mother's social security claims to take care of me. None of this was true, but it is where I was at the time. Sophomore year of high school, things hit the fan. I ended up being responsible for raising my younger brother, which I didn't feel was my job as a teenager. I had to abide by what I thought were these ridiculous rules, and I even had a curfew. Things like keeping my room clean and maintaining a good grade point average seemed like preposterous things to ask of a high school student. Now of course, as a high school student, I was very emotional about everything. But to my defense, at this time, I was just starting to process and deal with my mother's death. So, I was not in the best headspace to make things work. I tried to do everything in my power to do what was asked of me, but I was unable to get past my feelings of being neglected and abandoned.

I ended up leaving home and ventured out on my own, which left me homeless at times. I had to figure things out on my own. I needed some space. I needed clarity. I needed answers. When I left home, I didn't find a ton of answers, but I could ask a bunch of questions. I learned that asking questions helped me put things in perspective. I didn't need answers for everything. What I needed was someone to listen to me and be okay with me asking questions. I learned that as a parent, sometimes you carry a lot. And when you carry a lot on your shoulders, the last thing you want to do is answer a bunch of questions that your child keeps asking you. My father was carrying a lot and it wasn't his fault. He was just doing what he thought he was supposed to do. But because of that, he was unable to answer or even entertain the questions that I had. By not answering, it made me feel unwanted, alone, and helpless.

After a lot of time passed and I started my own family, I began to appreciate my father more. There was a lot that happened in between the time I left home and the time I started my family. There was work and healing that I had to do on myself. There was some reconciliation that I had to do with my father and I's relationship. Things never went back to the way they used to be, which was a great thing. We agreed to move as fast or slow as we needed, to be better men, and to have a better relationship.

Fast forward to today, he's one of my favorite people in the world. We have a great relationship. We are both still stubborn, so some things are better than others. But I finally feel like I really understand where he was coming from and why he made some of the decisions he made. This book is my reflections on some of those decisions, as well as me implementing things I've learned along the way. I hope you're able to take these things and apply them to life early or at least have the information stored in your head for use later. My father wasn't perfect, but he did his best. I'm not a perfect father, but I do my best. It is through his triumphs and mistakes, that I've been able to navigate life this far. Without him, I would not be the man that I am today. Without a loving father in my life, I don't know if I would be here today. My father drove me crazy most times during my adolescent years, but I'm mature to see that it wasn't him, it was me. Regardless of how I felt, regardless of the circumstance that he was in, he did the very best with what he could, when he could. That's what it means when I say Fathers Matter.

Respect

"Treat people the way you want to be treated. Talk to people the way you want to be talked to. Respect is earned, not given."

~ Hussein Nishah

Growing up my dad told me that I should be a man's man. He was a man's man. What is a man's man you ask? It's a man who will stand up and greet people face to face; A man who will look people in the eyes when they talk to them. A man's man gives out strong handshakes: he speaks to people with respect, meaning he speaks up clearly and directly; he gives people a confident response, so they know you mean what you say, he's honest by telling people what he can and cannot do for them. People just don't do that anymore these days.

People are scared to talk to people. Texting and social media has ruined how people communicate and socialize with each other. People are afraid to be honest with each other. People are scared to be real, honest, and transparent with each other. People don't want to tell others how they feel, instead, they take what we call in my hometown, the "Minnesota Nice" approach. "Minnesota Nice" is when you are passive aggressive and avoid having real conversations with each other. When you're being "Minnesota Nice", you use phrases like "interesting" and say things like "oh, is that so?" It's basically a form of being insincere, but you say it anyway to be nice and polite. People often use this approach when they don't want to stir the pot and create any confrontation. Things are a lot easier if you just follow through. My dad always taught me if you have respect, you never go back on your word; your word is your bond. You do what you say you're going to do. You show up, you help, and you care for others. You shovel your next-door neighbor's sidewalk. You cut their grass. You close their garage if left open. You do what you're supposed to do, even when you don't feel like it. These things all helped me to develop the confidence that I would need to be successful.

I developed confidence at an early age. My father made sure that I knew how to talk to people and how to show people respect. Growing up, I was always taught that looking someone in their eyes when they speak to you is a sign of respect. Once in elementary school, I got yelled at by a teacher because I looked him in the eyes. The teacher thought I was being rude and trying to be intimidating. I was just doing what my dad told me - look my teachers in their eyes when they are speaking to me. It shows that you are paying attention. It shows that you are listening. It shows that you care about what they are saying. It is a way of giving people respect and honor while they are talking to you. Having respect for people will help give others a great impression of you. You don't want people to think negative about you when someone mentions your name, and one way you can leave a positive impression on everyone, is by respecting them. Long after you are gone, people will associate your name with how you treated them. If you give and show people respect, your name will live on forever.

Notes

_____

_____

_____

_____

_____

_____

_____

_____

_____

_____

_____

_____

_____

_____

_____

_____

_____

Fathers Matter – Jesse Ross

Last Name

"Your name is the most important thing you own. Don't ever do anything to disgrace it or cheapen in." - Ben Hogan

My dad prides himself on having the last name Ross. He always told me that I was a Ross and that meant I had to walk in a room with confidence and walk in like I owned the building. This might sound crazy to you, but I used to watch my dad walk into rooms and just take over, but in a good way. He made everyone feel comfortable; he made everyone feel like they were important and that he actually cared about what was going on in their personal lives and not just in their professional lives. All too often, the word "networking" is used when people talk about a professional social gathering. That's not what my father taught me. My father taught me that networking was about getting to know someone and developing a genuine relationship with them.

My dad can walk in a room full of random people he doesn't know and by the time he leaves, he probably knows not only everyone's name in the room, but he also knows where they live, what school their kids attend, what kind of car they drive, and if he can help them do some work around their house. The man has the ability to make everyone feel like the party is just starting when he gets there, but he never wants to be the center of attention. Instead, he puts the attention on other people by making them feel important.

What I've learned from all this is the importance of being relational. When you build relationships with people, you care about how they will feel after you leave them. You should be intentional about the time you spend and the energy that you give other people.

Notes

_____

_____

_____

_____

_____

_____

_____

_____

_____

_____

_____

_____

_____

_____

_____

_____

_____

_____

_____

_____

_____

God & Family

Growing up, my dad always used to say that you need to know who God is. From my early memories of my childhood, I remember growing up and going to church. It seemed like we went to church every day. There was early service, bible study, choir meeting, deacon meeting, band meeting, afternoon service, revival, prayer service, watch night service, pre-watch night, after watch night service... You get the point. I even had to wear suits all the time.

With all that church, I noticed something. I noticed that a lot of men that were in the church were more in love with the idea of church than having a relationship with God. At the time, I didn't know what that meant, but my mother did her best to make sure that I knew exactly what having a relationship with Jesus meant.

If I could sum up two childhood lessons I was taught, I would pick:

1. Know *who* you are.

2. Know *whose* you are.

Who you are meant: you are a Ross, you represent your family, neighborhood, school, and yourself. Someone who is powerful. I represent black history and the prestige that should be carried with it. My African-American culture has helped me understand my identity in ways that I could not understand until I became older. Growing up in Minnesota, the large majority of the population is white. Being black was something that my mother made sure I was aware of. Whether it was how I behaved in the grocery store to what I wore anytime we left the house, to the elders that she made sure I was around. My mother was very intentional about teaching me that my culture was something I would constantly be reminded of, whether I wanted to or not. My heritage consists of Egyptian Kings and Queens; therefore, I was taught that I should carry myself in that manner. I was taught that it did not matter if the people around me treated me like a king, if I treated myself as such, then I could rest knowing that I had to confidence to conquer anything in front of me.

Whose you are meant: you're my son. My mother and father used to say things like "you better not embarrass me" and "bet not get out there and act a fool". They emphasized this because my mom was well known in the community. She was good friends with the mayor and other elected officials. So not only was her reputation at stake if I did something crazy, but my family's reputation as well. My mother was a no-nonsense type of person. She taught me that everything that is done in the dark, comes to light. That was her way of teaching me to be honest. Somehow, she would always find out what I was doing or had done before I had the chance to tell her. She wanted me to acknowledge and take ownership of my own actions as a young boy, so that when I got older, it was already a healthy habit. I believe we were all created to do something and to do good in the world. But there is no way that we are able to do good work in the world, if we don't take care of the little things. My attitude and behavior was the first thing that my mom tried to teach me to self-assess.

My mother taught me the importance of God and family. That was ingrained in me from day one. My father taught me to always take care of family. To me, family is like the cards of life that you are dealt, and you pretty much have to play them. There aren't too many changes you can make when it comes to your family. However, you still get a choice in how you play. We can pick and choose how we play those cards and for what. Some people use family for money. Others see family as a support system. Some people see their families as leverage just to say they are related to someone famous or for social recognition. Some people use family for prestige, and still others use family to gain access to places.

Family also includes the people that have no genetic relationship to you. I learned from my dad that it didn't matter if you were a friend or close neighbor. If you came to our house, you were considered family. I learned to value friendship and the time and effort it takes to invest in those relationships.

My dad gave me a great example of this principle. One day, he was thinking about buying some furniture, so he called my uncle Ron and uncle Earl to come help him "try out the furniture". Having never heard of such a thing, I asked my dad, "Why are you having them try out the furniture?" His response was, "It's not all about me, and not all about you. They are on the couch more than I am. If it's comfortable for them, then it's definitely comfortable me and for everyone else."

Wow. I never thought about it that way. Here he was buying his own home and taking care of his family, but he was thinking about the people that will come over, the people who will come to talk with my parents about their problems and the people that will eventually come over and eat. My dad was thinking about how important it was to make his friends feel good when he bought the furniture and they would know that they played a major role in a lasting decision for my dad. He taught me that people are important to God, so they should be important to you.

Notes

Fathers Matter – Jesse Ross

Character

"Solid character will reflect itself in consistent behavior, while poor character will seek to hide behind deceptive words and actions.

~ *Myles Monroe*

Your character is something that follows you everywhere you go. My dad used to say, "Son, don't let material things destroy or corrupt your character, or get it out of sync." What he meant by that was the more you work, the more money you make, the more you must buy and spend. When you spend money, it makes you feel like you are important. Not that you should not feel important, but his point was do not let the money and your inflated ego give you false hope. Prioritizing what you care about should be important to you. Money and material things have the potential to inflate your ego; because you bought this thing of value, you feel like you're better than everyone else.

When your character is out of whack, you run the risk of becoming disrespectful. You don't want to start thinking you are better than everyone, just because you think you've become this important person. Instead, a better idea is to figure out how to use your resources to ensure that we all succeed. You shouldn't let status get to our head. Stay level headed. Take care of people and don't worry. It'll all work out in the end.

Notes

_____

_____

_____

_____

_____

_____

_____

_____

_____

_____

_____

_____

_____

_____

_____

_____

_____

_____

_____

_____

_____

Fathers Matter – Jesse Ross

Income: Primary vs Secondary

"He who makes $25,000 annually through passive income is more enviable than he who earns $100,000 annually through a salary."

— Mokokoma Mokhonooana

This refers to work or whatever you call your main source of income. My dad always said everyone should have a primary source of income. Fortunately, I've never known my dad to be without a job at any point in his life. As a matter of fact, he's always had more than one job. In his day, there was no "oh I'm done with my work, going to leave everything at the office until tomorrow."

The work ethic I have, I got from him. Growing up, I saw my father get up and go to work every day, Monday through Saturday. He would get up early, go to work at his primary job and when he got off from that job he would then go work on someone's car, go fix a deck, paint a garage, or help someone remodel their basement.

My dad always had a hustle. That was his second-ary income. He always made sure there was some money he could make with his hands. "Son, always be able to do something with your hands," He would say to me. "That way, they can never take it away from you." My dad was a welder by trade, but he was also a good mechanic. He tried to get me to work on cars, but I hated it. It was hard work and it was dirty. I loved and admired the skill though. I loved that you could take something apart and put it back together. Although he loved to do it, I just didn't want to get dirty all day. I wanted to do something that allowed me to think critically. Little did I know, I picked up a ton just by watching him. I still don't like it to this day. I hate working on cars but I know how to do some basic maintenance if I need to get it done. I know plenty of men that do not know how to change a tire. My father made sure that I knew how to change a tire, change my breaks and oil. He wanted to make sure I knew the basics.

Working on cars was definitely not my calling, but I loved cutting hair. I learned everything about cutting hair from my cousin, Little James. I even went to barber school for a short period. When I wasn't at barber school,

I would sit and watch him over and over, until I had to go to bed or somewhere else and over time, I picked up how to cut hair. One day a few of my friends needed to get their hair cut but there were no openings at the local barbershops. So, I grabbed a pair of clippers and tried my hand and it worked out. If I had stayed in barber school I probably could have owned several shops by now.

In my lifetime, I have had full-time jobs and a few part-time jobs. One of my part time jobs was singing. I used to lead worship for a church, but nobody knew it was a side gig. I used to sing background vocals for other people, be guests at local churches, and I would even travel around to different events or conferences just to make a little money on the side.

What is your secondary income? If you don't have one, you should develop one. Find something else besides your primary source of income that you are good at doing. Some people drive for Uber or Lyft. Some people work overnight shifts at hotels or shelters. The options are limitless.

But before looking for a part time job, make sure you have solid full time employment first. Take care of the responsibilities in front of you before you decide to work on a side hustle. And when you do start to work on your side hustle, have a plan. Some people like their side hustle more than they like their fulltime job, which is okay. The goal is for you to get to a point where you can do what you want to do. To get to that place you're going to have to work hard to achieve your goals.

Notes

_____

_____

_____

_____

_____

_____

_____

_____

_____

_____

_____

_____

_____

_____

_____

_____

_____

_____

_____

_____

_____

Fathers Matter – Jesse Ross

Integrity

"Integrity is choosing courage over comfort; choosing what's right over what is fun, fast, or easy; and choosing to practice our values rather than simply processing them."

~ Brene Brown

There comes a time in a person's life where they must stand up for something. We are influenced by so many different things in life. So many things are trying to infiltrate our culture, beliefs, and mindset. These things take us, and try to force us to become what they are, not who we were created to be. My father always taught me to stand up for people and remember who you are and whose you are. He told me that part of being a man meant that you believe in the people around you and also protect everyone around you.

You might be asking, "what do you mean protect and whom?" Everything and everyone. Your community, your family, loved ones, your friends, little children, homeless people, elderly people, the person who cannot protect themselves. Everyone. My dad used to talk to me a lot about living in this world filled with images of false masculinity. In the world that I grew up in, men were considered men when they fight, harm, shoot, or kill other men. My father taught me that killing and destroying a person's life is a false narrative of what a real man should look like. We live in a time where the media portrays arguing, yelling, and being controlling as examples of being a man. Now this isn't all of media, of course. But pay attention next time you're watching an action movie and see what you notice. We live in a time where masculinity means walking around with your shirt off and poking your chest out because you have muscles.

These, and plenty of other images, are examples of false masculinity that I want you to stand up against. Stand up against the false pretenses and images that plague our culture, environment, schools, families, and communities. Stand up for the young lady who doesn't have a dad, a brother, cousins, and uncles around to stand up for her. Stand up for her as she walks through your school hallways. Stand up when the bullies or brats try to tease her about how she dresses, her weight, her hair, or self-esteem. Whether she's on her way home, or she's on her way to school or she's on her way to the store, just look out for her. Don't let these chumps take advantage of her beauty. Don't let them fuel her thoughts with imperfect or false ideas of beauty. Please, don't let them take advantage of her.

When I was going through my divorce, my dad asked me if I believed in my heart that I did what I could to make things right and reconcile. When I told him yes, he said that was all that matters, and to stand by that. He encouraged me to stand by my values and my beliefs. People will fade, people will wither away, and people will dry out. People will either move on, move away, or move back. But your beliefs and your value system will keep you firm and rooted in what's right. Not only in what you were created to be, but in your community, as well as in your family. It keeps you rooted in life. Stand strong and stand up.

This reminds me of another situation. I was in a meeting at work one day a few years ago, and there were quite a few women and only two men. During the meeting, one of the men got defensive after one of the women made a comment. He decided that he was going to exercise his power, control, manhood, in response to her comment. He stood up, and tried to intimidate her. I reacted by telling him that he needed to chill out. Now this isn't to say that I'm this great guy, but I believe that we need more men that are willing to stand up in situations like those and speak out. Not to rescue women, because women are beyond capable of taking care of themselves, but rather, we as men ought to be present to assist in navigating situations like that. When men take advantage of people and use their power for evil, we need more superhero Clark Kent like men who will step up, men who will be men and hold other men accountable.

Notes

_____

_____

_____

_____

_____

_____

_____

_____

_____

_____

_____

_____

_____

_____

_____

_____

_____

_____

_____

_____

Fathers Matter – Jesse Ross

Celebrated, not Tolerated

"People may not always be able to see the treasure God has placed within you, so don't place too much value on the opinion of others. Trust that God knows what's in you, and He will choose you, even when others overlook you." ~ Unknown

This is something I learned while working at a previous job where I spent a significant time of my life. I worked there for several years and enjoyed my job. The people I got to work with locally and across the country were amazing. The young people I got to work with were amazing, and I continue to keep in contact with a lot of them. But I realized after a while that as I was trying to grow and develop more skills, I wasn't being celebrated and appreciated the way I felt I should've been. I thought I was being celebrated, but I was only being tolerated. I thought it was my dream job at the time. Who wouldn't want a job where you get to hang out with kids, and be in schools building relationships with people in the community? It was something I loved to do. But as time went on, I began to see that I was not being celebrated. I wasn't being promoted. I wasn't being acknowledged for the work that I accomplished. And I ignored those signs for a long time because I enjoyed my job. It was never about the credit or accolades. But I realized that I only got trained and developed if it was required or if I pushed for it to happen. They tolerated me. They tolerated my ideas and aspirations. They tolerated my urban swag. They tolerated my ability to use music to capture teenagers. They tolerated my ability to see the good in people when they didn't see the good in themselves. People will use you for their own good if you let them.

In the long run, I learned to remember this going into every situation. Going where you're celebrated, means that you go where people are consistently trying to develop you, pour into you, and create opportunities for you. They don't stunt your growth, regardless of their ability to train you. They will seek out opportunities for you. They will push you and challenge you and tell you when you are not doing something right. And they are not out to embarrass you, but to make you better and help you grow.

If you are in situations where people don't challenge you, where you aren't growing, where you aren't getting opportunities to expand and develop your skills or add new skills, that means you could be in a situation where you are being tolerated and not celebrated. If you feel like you don't belong, you are definitely being tolerated. My dad told me that he never went to a place where he didn't feel welcomed. I never understood it until later in life. Remember, he is an African-American man from Mississippi. He knew that not everyone in the world would appreciate him, and he was perfectly okay with that.

I mean think about it. Why would I go somewhere I'm not welcomed? In our history, there have been times where people who were perceived as "different" were not allowed in certain venues and facilities. Some purposely made it their mission to keep the *different* folks out. When you go somewhere you are celebrated, be it college, church, organizations, girls' night out, certain group of friends, workplace, etc., you want to be in a place that values your expertise and opinions. You want to feel like you serve a purpose in that group or place. You can feel the difference, too. You can feel the love, the welcome, you feel invited, you don't feel like someone will steal all your ideas, and you don't have the underlying feeling of "why am I here?"

Notes

_____

_____

_____

_____

_____

_____

_____

_____

_____

_____

_____

_____

_____

_____

_____

_____

_____

Gentlemen

"A gentleman is not defined by the contents of his wallet or the cut of his suit. He is defined by his manners and the content of his character."

~ Unknown

I have had many debates with women I know about whether chivalry is dead, or alive, or missing in action somewhere. I know a lot of women who feel like chivalry is buried six feet under in Montana somewhere. No offense if you're reading this and live in or are from Montana. I never thought about chivalry being dead because I was raised to be a gentleman, always, not just on Sundays. I was taught that you open doors, say please and thank you, or may I? I was taught you compliment people genuinely, not just making something up because it sounds good. When you meet someone, you make sure you are standing.

"Clowns and frowns I meet in their seat, but real men, I meet on their feet." That's something my dad used to say all the time. It basically means you were frowned upon if you did not stand up to meet someone. I was taught to do little things like opening the door, whether it's for a man or a woman, but especially for a woman. It's just polite to let people to go in first. When you're getting onto an elevator or getting off, you allow people to go in front of you. When you're walking on the street, you walk on the side that is closest to cars driving. You are the shield in case something happens. These are things I grew up being taught.

Some of these things I learned from my mother also. She didn't want her little boy growing up in this world without any manners, or as they say in the south, "home training". Maybe that's it. Maybe people don't have any home training anymore. My mother wanted me to be someone that people liked and respected. She wanted me to be the one that parents wanted to introduce their daughters to in high school, simply because I was a gentleman, and they knew their daughter would be safe with me.

My father wanted me to be a gentleman because he knew it would take me places. Someone once told me a story about a man who owned a grocery store who always hired people that were polite but had very little cashier or customer service experience. One day, someone asked him, "Why do you hire all these people who don't have any of the skills that we need?" He responded, "You know, I hire nice people because you can teach nice people to do anything. But you can't teach people to be nice and polite to customers." That has always stuck with me. Be polite. Be respectful. Include people. Make people feel important. Be respectful. Make sure people don't feel left out. You can teach people all kinds of skills and management. You can't teach people to be polite. You can teach a boy to be a gentleman.

Earlier, I talked about living in a day where false masculinity is destroying our society. Being a gentleman isn't just about opening doors, it's about being considerate of others. It is thinking about how well you can treat someone, whether you know them or not. How much value can you add to someone's life?

Think about this. The time that you spend with people, is it worth it? Is it worth it to you or them? Do you ever feel like, after having lunch or coffee with someone, energized or are you drained? When people spend time with you, do they walk away saying that they enjoy spending time with you? Or do they feel like, "Man, that was cool, but I would've rather been doing XYZ." I hope and pray that when we decide to allocate our resources of time, talent, and treasure, we leave people and places better than when we found them. When people spend time with you, they should realize that, not only were you nice, polite, and a gentleman, but that you added value to their life. They should immediately be looking forward to the next time they get to see you.

The reason why people should look forward to the next time they interact with you is because your presence should enlighten people, energize them, and make them feel important.

Notes

Work ethic

"Hard work without consistency will lead you nowhere." - Unknown

My father taught me how to work hard and how to be persistent. He taught me how to get the job done, and do it the right way the first time. He was in the military, so he was very particular about the way things were done and the order in which they were done. It used to drive me insane! He was picky about me making my bed every morning. Personally, I felt like if all I'm going to do is lay right back in my bed later when I get home, why should I make it? But my father felt strongly about making your bed every morning. He felt like it gave you a sense of order in the morning. For instance, the first things you should do in the morning are brush your teeth, wash your face, take a shower (if not the night before), put lotion and deodorant on, make your bed, and get dressed. It's just how he did things, and he expected us to follow suit.

I would definitely say that my work ethic comes

from both my mother and my father, but, because my mother passed away when I was younger, I only remember glimpses of her work ethic. She was a thinker, some would say a strategist. She was a person who would hustle, but she was always thinking about efficiency. She tried to figure out how to spend the least amount of energy, but get the most results. My father always had a hustle though. Don't get it twisted. This guy worked all the time. He worked on cars, and he was a handyman. One day I came home from school and he had completely torn down the deck. I asked him what he was doing, and he told me he randomly decided he wanted to build a new deck. He was always somewhere helping at the church. He just did the most with what he had to make things work.

I watched my dad get up every single day to go to work and he worked every shift they gave him: Overtime, weekends, early mornings, it didn't matter. And he went to work every single day. In high school, I got perfect attendance because of him. He never knew it, but I went to school every day. Now I know what you are thinking. Doesn't everyone go to school every day? You'd be surprised at how many people you know that don't go to

Fathers Matter – Jesse Ross

school every day. I know you're supposed to go every day, but let's be for real. I didn't go to school every day just because I had to, but it was really because I saw him do it. He just worked and showed up as much as he could. That was what he did, so it's what I did. Your work ethic can be taught and learned, and it always beats talent. You should be able to outwork and outhustle smart people. I take that back. You should be willing to outwork and outhustle anyone.

Notes

Raising Daughters

"A girl's father should be the greatest example of how a man should treat a lady. She should expect the best and not accept anything less." ~ Unknown

When the time comes, take care of your daughters. Ironically, my father also taught me how to love on my daughters. When my daughter was born, she instantly became the love of my life. I cannot explain accurately how excited I was when I found out that I was having a girl. Now, if you ask my stepmom, she will be real honest and tell you that I always wanted a black chocolate baby doll. Black as charcoal. Black like the night. I wanted a daughter so black that if you put lotion on her, she'd shine like tires out of a fresh car wash. When she was born, it was like my entire world changed and it took on a whole new meaning. My father taught me in a roundabout way how to take care of my children because he had to step up to the challenge when my birth mother passed.

My mother passed when I was 11 years old. At the

time my father and I didn't have a great relationship, but he stepped in anyway. For that, and so many other countless things he has done for me, I'm grateful. I don't know what it would be like growing up without my father. My daughter is one of the most important gifts that I've ever received in my life. I don't know what I would do or be without experiencing her birth into this world. I've learned how to be patient. I've learned to continue to let her know that her black is beautiful. I have learned to empower her and let her know that she can do anything in this world that she sets her mind to, and I'll be right beside her to help her navigate whatever may come her way. I'm here to let her know she's not too girly to play a sport, she's not too soft to play with the boys, she's not too small, skinny, or tall, and her hair is not funny or weird. Her black is beautiful. It's so important that daughters have their fathers in their lives. It's even more important that as they grow into young girls, they have fathers in their lives. Young girls need to understand that their father will do anything and hurt anyone who stands in the way of their daughter reaching her goals. Now, of course, I am not promoting violence by any means. I am

Fathers Matter – Jesse Ross

just trying to make a point. I'm so thankful for my daughter. I'm thankful that God has allowed me the opportunity to be renewed and transformed by her presence. I've learned how to communicate better because of her. I've learned how to make sure that I show her unconditional love and let her know that she can conquer the world.

Notes

Raising Sons

"You're not raising your son, you're raising someone's husband, and someone's father... So, raise him well!" - *Unknown*

What I learned from my father about raising sons is that you have to let boys grow. Let him be what he's going to be and do what he's going to do. Being a boy means he's going to get into stuff and be hard headed. It's pretty much inevitable. He's going to explore, tear up some stuff, build, crash, make noise, yell, wrestle, and anything else you can think of. You have to let young boys grow and wrestle. Wrestling doesn't just represent a physical challenge to them. Wrestling affords them the opportunity to process that sometimes you must think your way through situations, not just use your brute strength.

I learned from my father that discipline is an art. It has to be well thought out. You must talk to your sons. You have to get on their level and maintain a healthy balance of respect and Godly fear, but not demoralize their pride and sense of self identity. My father taught me that you must work through and process what things went wrong, why they went wrong, how we can avoid these things going wrong in the future. We must help boys think critically and process how to make better decisions the next time around.

My dad made sure that he empowered me also. He told me that I could be anything that I ever wanted to be, but I had to be willing to put in the work. Even when I thought he was crazy, I still believed it, because he believed it. I believed that I could be a fighter jet pilot or the president of the United States, mainly because my father told me I could and believed I could!

In my son's life, I realize the importance that I play in shaping him. It is such an important role. I know so many young boys and so many of my friends growing up that grew up with only their mothers. Now hear me, there is absolutely nothing wrong with women raising young men. That's not my point. There is something wrong with that situation. What's wrong about it is a mother should not have to do it by herself. Once again, there's nothing wrong with women raising young men, but clearly there's a need for the presence of men in the lives of their children. They need mothers, but they also need fathers. Children need a father's presence as a role model. It is very important in the development of a young man, especially in shaping the lives of young African American boys like my son.

Sometimes I'm convinced that my son thinks I'm superman. On most days, he probably thinks that I can do anything. Literally. When I come home and kiss him and hug him and pray over him at night, I'm developing healthy practices with him. Hopefully, in the future, he will grow up and develop his own practices. I'm not only shaping his world, but I'm shaping my future grandchildren's world. I'm shaping his school and neighborhood friend's world. I represent more than just me. I represent an image for young boys that need to know that they are strong and can stand up to anything in the world. But also, that they are one of the most dangerous creations known to man. If they can figure out how to harness their energy in the right direction, the opportunities for their future are limitless.

Notes

Relationships

"Surround yourself with the dreamers and doers, the believers and thinkers. But, most of all, surround yourself with those who see greatness within you." ~ Unknown

Relationships are important because you never know who you might meet and who you might need. My father used to tell me that you should never throw a phone number away. I have somewhere around 5,332 contacts in my phone. You never throw a contact away. Relationships can get you into a school, keep you out of trouble, keep you in school, or someone may have something that you need. Growing up with my mother, she emphasized how important relationships are by how she lived her life. She always told me to make sure I take care of people. Not because it's my responsibility to them, but it was my responsibility to God. She always used to say people are important to God, so they should be important to us. You show how much you value your relationships with people when you spend time and energy with them. Those are the things that people cannot put a price tag on. You make people feel important and make people feel welcomed. You make people feel like they are not in it by themselves. You never know who you might need, so make sure you keep track of your relationships. Maybe you should do some inventory on your relationships one day.

Relationships can work both ways. Some relationships are toxic. For some reason, you can feel like people owe you something or you feel obligated to be their friend. Sometimes you even feel obligated to not cut or release them out of our lives. People will suck your time dry and waste it if you allow them to. Those are the people who will continuously nag the hell out you.

There is also so much goodness that can come from being in the right healthy relationships/friendships with people. When you are around the right people, you can see things clicking in other areas of your life. When you are in healthy relationships, you feel like people know you so well and you can see the value that they add to your life. These people help you navigate situations without feeling like you are bothering them. They offer their opinions when asked, not just because they want to be nosey. When you get around the right friendships, you get the opportunity to see some things in yourself that you wouldn't see had you not been with them.

My dad used to say that you are the sum of the company you keep. Meaning, if I'm hanging around with people who don't care about school that much, more than likely I'm not going to care about school that much. If I'm friends with athletes, I'm more than likely going to be an athlete. If most of the friends in my circle have degrees or advanced degrees, I'm more than likely going to at least think about obtaining an advanced degree. You are the sum of the company you keep. Do your best to identify the people in your life that you want to be around, and spend time building those relationships. I promise you'll see the pay off in the long run.

Fathers Matter – Jesse Ross

Notes

Fathers Matter – Jesse Ross

Fathers Matter – Jesse Ross

Image is Everything

~ *Unknown*

People look at you and in the first five to seven seconds, they judge you. They either say you aren't worth their time, you're weird, that you look funny, or you are worth their time. Image and presentation is everything. I was always told that people are watching my every move. Now, as an athlete in high school, this was really important. Even though I wasn't Division 1 material, schools were still watching me. Some teams weren't looking for the best scoring prospect on every trip. Some coaches were looking for a kid who they didn't have to watch 24/7. Some coaches were looking for a kid who wouldn't mind sitting on the bench. Some coaches were looking for kids who they knew would go to class every day and make the grades and stay eligible throughout the season.

Remember, my dad always told me to make sure that I look people in the eyes when they spoke to me. Acknowledge them. Show you're interested. There are times when we don't want to be judged by what we wear or how we look, but the reality is, that's the world we live in. I'm guilty of it, you're guilty. We are all guilty. So, make sure you pay attention to what you wear and how you dress.

I used to see people going outside all the time in pajamas, slippers, and du-rags and I used to feel so bad for them. The last thing I wished was for them to run into their future employer; a potential job opportunity, their next coach, their next mentor, their future spouse or business partner, they miss the opportunity. Presentation is everything. If you wanted to impress a businessman, but you don't dress well when you meet him, the businessman might not give you the job. And if I don't get the job, that means I might not be able to provide for my family. And, if I can't provide for my family, that means we have a problem. Nobody wants to be judged, but the reality is, we all judge. So, do your best to take care of yourself, take care of your image, and make sure you are putting forth the effort to be the best version of you as possible. Yes, it takes a little bit of work, but is it worth it in the long run? Definitely.

Notes

_____

_____

_____

_____

_____

_____

_____

_____

_____

_____

_____

_____

_____

_____

_____

_____

_____

Having kids

"Your children don't have to come from you. They go through you."
-Unknown

Having a child is one of the most beautiful things that could ever happen to anyone. As fathers, we long for a way to duplicate ourselves. We long for a way to pass down lessons and tricks and tips that we've learned. We long to share those lessons with whoever is willing to listen. When you have a child that's one way you can pass those down. It's one of the most humbling experiences you can have in your life. There are times when you are scared as hell! Like the first day we took home my daughter from the hospital. I literally did not know what to do. I remember when we walked in the house and I sat the car seat down on the floor and she was sleep. Sleeping so peacefully but inside my head I was thinking "what am I I going to do when she woke up?" There are times in your life, when you wish you had a manual, and there are times when you have it all together. It constantly reminds me to push. Push past the hurt. Push past the pain. Past the feelings. It reminds me to think about someone other than myself.

Mentoring is also another way to build into the lives of children and pass on lessons. I know people who have many "spiritual" children, without having to birth their own. Every child needs someone who can help them go through life's joys and challenges. There are so many opportunities to connect with young people in the schools, parks, after-school programs, and countless volunteer youth-focused organizations.

Notes

Fathers Matter – Jesse Ross

Fathers Matter – Jesse Ross

Sacrifice

"If you don't sacrifice for what you want, what you want will be the sacrifice." - Unknown

How much are you willing to sacrifice to get where you want to be in life? My father taught me this lesson by modeling it. He sacrificed sleep, material things and his spare time to make sure that his family was taken care of. To provide for your family, you are going to have to sacrifice. I watched my dad buy a car that wasn't the greatest, fix it up, sell it, then buy another car that was just a step up from the last one, fix it up, and sell it. Then buy another car again, and fix it up, and sell it again. I watched him do this over and over until he got to the car he wanted and enjoyed. This wasn't because he really enjoyed that whole process. He just knew the value of sacrifice. Sacrifice the immediate gratification in order to achieve what you want in the long run.

My father couldn't stand owing anyone anything. If he didn't have it cash, he wasn't going to get it. He would find different ways to keep his costs down. He would find boosters. Boosters are people who would just happen to find random items on normal occasions that would have exactly what you need during back to school seasons. Or when the seasons changed and you needed some clothes for the season. When it was time to get groceries, my dad would pay someone to buy their food stamps. He paid half the cost of what he would have spent at the grocery store. My dad kept one or two people like that in his life at all times. This wasn't because he was trying to cheat the system, but it was him trying to figure out how to make sure he kept some money in his pocket. Luckily, I went to a school that had a uniform, so we didn't need to worry about clothes as often as my other non-uniform friends. They would have to go shopping over summer break. We didn't have to worry about that, so I got to save all that money I made over the summer.

Notes

Fathers Matter – Jesse Ross

Fathers Matter – Jesse Ross

Create opportunities

"It isn't sufficient just to want – you've got to ask yourself what you are going to do to get to the things you want."

~ *Franklin D. Roosevelt*

Opportunities come to those who create them. This is something that took me a while to really understand because the world we live in, you can create anything you want, but you have to "pull yourself up by your bootstraps." I didn't even know what that really meant until it I heard people talking about it as it relates to politics and capitalism. My father taught me that if you want something, you have to go get it. And if it hasn't been done before, that doesn't mean that it can't be done, but you're going to have to create it.

I remember there were a couple times in my career where I ran a few programs, and there were certain "way we've always done things". In this case, I was new, came in, and asked a bunch of questions. Why did we do this? Why don't we do this? What's the reason behind this?

And people had a problem with it. I wasn't asking questions to be arrogant or to be difficult. But what I found out is that they had been missing opportunities to expand and grow the program. When you keep doing the same things repeatedly, you miss opportunities to expand capacity and maximize success. Had I not been in the meetings going forward and asked questions, we might not have been able to get additional funding for the programs. If I didn't ask those questions, we probably wouldn't have expanded our number of participants in the program, and we would've missed out on the impact. You have to create your own opportunities.

Are you willing to go against the status quo and go for what you want in life? Are you willing to spend every minute, hour, day you have at your disposal going after that goal or dream? Every moment can be daunting, I'm sure. BUT I THINK IT'S POSSIBLE. It's doable. It takes effort. Maybe it's an hour a day. There has to be some dedication. You have to be okay with offending people. Nobody is going to create an opportunity for you. There are a limited number of people who will open a door for you. There are plenty of people, however, that will make sure doors not only close, but that they lock on you. What are some opportunities that you can create so that you can be what you want to be? What are things you can't see because your environment?

What environments do you need to get out of or into, so you can start to create?

Notes

Fathers Matter – Jesse Ross

Fathers Matter – Jesse Ross

Sleep is overrated

"Someday, when you least expect it, you will be called on to serve. Prepare yourself. Develop skill. Learn to master your craft. Be ready for that call."

~ *Brenden Burchard*

I learned a long time ago that while the rest of my friends were sleeping, if I was working, or working out, or just being productive, I could get the jump on them. People love to sleep. But for me, it's something that I realized I don't need a ton of. I'm also willing to sacrifice sleep in order to get to the level I'm trying to get to. I realized I don't need eight hours of sleep. I take five. I get up in the morning. Read. I make the kids breakfast. I do voice recordings. I make lunches. I get emails done for work. Spend time in devotion. Work out. It's not creating a habit of being a workaholic. It's about valuing my own goals and wanting to reach them. Either I'll be sleep and be lazy, or I'll get up and work on my dreams until I am where I say I want to be. There is no way I'm going to let sleep stand in the way of getting to my dreams.

Notes

_____

_____

_____

_____

_____

_____

_____

_____

_____

_____

_____

_____

_____

_____

_____

_____

_____

Fathers Matter – Jesse Ross

Mentor

"A lot of people have gone further than they thought they could because someone else thought they could"

-Unknown

Overtime, my father taught to always have a mentor. It's a way to get better at certain things. You can have a mentor in pretty much anything. Whether it be finances, exercise, work related, or just a random hobby.

It's not just this person you idolize and adore. Having a mentor should represent you wanting to get better and understanding that you can't do it alone. If you have a mentor, or when you have one, the main purpose is to help you get better in various areas of your life. A role of a mentor is to give you advice in areas that you have not yet mastered. You should be asking your mentor to help you in your areas of weakness. It is as simple as saying to someone, "Hey, I need help learning this new skill, would you mind meeting with me or pointing me in the right direction?"

If you have a mentor, you should also at the same time be mentoring someone else. You should simultaneously be expanding and passing down the knowledge you have received to someone else. You can do that by seeking out wisdom, then passing down wisdom.

Some of the wisdom you receive is not just meant for you. Some of the wisdom you receive isn't meant for you at all. You have to funnel all that stuff. Park the info that you need to pass on and apply the information that is specifically for you. But you have to make sure you pass that on as well. Pass on the info that you feel like could help your mentee be successful. Whether we are being mentored or have a mentee, it helps us grow personally. No one is too old to have a mentor. My father always had people in his life that knew different skills than him. I never understood why he'd share a garage with a guy down the street from us. My father would use this man's garage for doing his different projects, but all three men worked on the projects. It was a way of keeping them fresh and to learn something that wasn't their area of expertise.

Fathers Matter – Jesse Ross

I hope you aren't the smartest person in the room. If you are the smartest person in your friend group, you may need to get some new friends. Never settle and always be willing to grow. There are opportunities that come to us all the time that give us space to grow and sometimes, we need to grow by offering things. Sometimes we just need to be present. What are the areas in your life that you need a mentor? In which areas, can you be a mentor? And what are doing in that space? What's stopping you?

Notes

_____

_____

_____

_____

_____

_____

_____

_____

_____

_____

_____

_____

_____

_____

_____

_____

_____

_____

_____

_____

_____

_____

_____

Respect and Honor your elders

"Respect your elders. Learn from the people who have walked the path before you…respect them. Because someday, and sooner than you can imagine, you are going to grow old too." - Unknown

What is your connection to the elders around you and your community? Fortunately for me, my dad was always one of the older guys in the group. Since he was a little older, he hung out with guys that were a little older than him. I used to sit and watch these older men fix cars and do different house projects every other weekend. It seemed like every car in our neighborhood had at one point visited our garage. What I remember most about these moments were the stories that they shared. Stories about dealing with healthy marriages, divorce, kids getting older, trying to find different jobs, and dealing with their health issues from time to time. These conversations provided opportunities for me to listen, learn, and pick up so much knowledge that I never knew would come in handy later. Being around these older guys also

Fathers Matter – Jesse Ross

helped me understand how things happened in the community.

One well known pastor used to come by all the time and have my dad look at his cars. This pastor was someone who ended up looking out for me when I happened to be in a situation hanging out with the wrong people. The pastor stopped me from getting into a fight with some guys. He told the guys that I was a good kid, to leave me alone, and he took me home to make sure that I got there safely.

I don't think these types of conversations and relationships happen anymore between the elders in our community and young people. Something happened that created a distance between the two. I hope one day we can get back to the "good ole days", where we talked as a community and passed on information to each other. I do have an idea about how the distance was created.

I heard this former BET correspondent, Jeff Johnson, tell a story about the difference between elders and old people. Old people believe that their time on the earth was just about them. They are and have been selfish pretty much their whole lives. They are scared to live any more than they already have. Worst of all, they believe young people are there only to take their spot.

Elders on the other hand, believe that young people are purposed to be great. They believe their responsibility is to pour into the younger generation to make the next generation better. They believe that they should make the world a better place for those that come after them.

Sometimes honoring and respecting our elders is very hard. Believe me, I know how hard it is. But it's worth it. I always think about how I want someone to treat me when I get old. I want people to feel like I've earned their respect because of the impact I've had on their lives. I want people to know that I care about them and hopefully they care about me enough to spend some time with me so I can learn. There is a lot of wisdom in elders. They have so much wisdom sometimes that it can help us avoid getting many bumps and bruises on our heads when it comes to life.

Fathers Matter – Jesse Ross

Notes

_____

_____

_____

_____

_____

_____

_____

_____

_____

_____

_____

_____

_____

_____

_____

_____

_____

Fathers Matter – Jesse Ross

Nothing lasts forever

"We get one opportunity in life, one chance at life to do whatever you're going to do, and lay your foundation and make whatever mark you're going to make. Whatever legacy you're going to leave, leave it!" – Ray Lewis

Growing up, my father was around sometimes and other times not so much. In my child mind, that was my fault or my mother's fault. It took me a while to really understand his side of the story. He didn't really know how to be a present father. He was just in the moment. And he was trying to figure it out. When I say, nothing lasts forever, that means that nothing in this world is guaranteed. We all have a date when we are born, and all have a date when we will die.

In high school, I ran away from home at age fifteen. I had so much going on at the time, but I was mainly dealing with my mother's death from five years prior. My dad wasn't a great dad at the time; he was still learning. Those moments were real for me; feeling hurt and pain, and feeling abandoned. All those things I felt at the time were real, but nothing lasts forever. The hurt and pain that was created between me and my father after I left home, that was real. Some days I didn't feel like picking up the phone when it rang and sometimes that feeling would last anywhere from a few hours to a few days to as long as a few months. Those feelings and emotions were real. But nothing lasts forever.

I discovered that my father had prostate cancer in 2016. He pretty much fumbled his way through telling me over a six-month period, then things became real. I was all the way in Minneapolis, MN, and I couldn't get to him in Charlotte, NC. I thought about all the doctors' visits and treatment meetings that I had to miss. Those were real. But nothing lasts forever.

I'm here to encourage you that things are hard. Life is hard. Things are difficult, they hurt, and those things are all real. But nothing lasts forever.

I'm at a point in my life where right now, if I lost him, I'd be devastated. It would hurt deep. Not just because of who he is right now, but because of what he means to me. I'd want more time and more opportunities

Fathers Matter – Jesse Ross

to listen and learn. I'd want more time just to be with him. But nothing last forever. Life doesn't and won't stop just for me. It would kill me thinking about all the things we have yet to talk about or do together or navigate. One thing that he said he wants to do before he dies is take a trip to NYC. It's my goal to make that happen.

If you're reading this book, I want to encourage you to love hard. To be present. To forgive. To have fun. To enjoy life and enjoy people and their presence. Do everything you can to make a difference. Understand people are important. Be a gentleman. Take care of each other. And always remember, that nothing lasts forever.

Notes

_____

_____

_____

_____

_____

_____

_____

_____

_____

_____

_____

_____

_____

_____

_____

Fathers Matter – Jesse Ross

ABOUT THE AUTHOR

Jesse is an Author, Speaker, & Professional Development Coach. Jesse's work stems from his deep passion for people and communities. He works to guide people in effectively impacting their own communities – both in their work-place and beyond. His work focuses on a range of topics falling under categories of diversity and culture, youth and family development, and leadership focus.

Fathers Matter – Jesse Ross

Bring the Fathers Matters Tour to Your Town

Jesse Ross is available to come to your city for book signings and events. Jesse is skilled at providing unique, inspiring, and effective keynote presentations and workshops for audiences of all sizes. Want to book Jesse for an event, conference, workshop, or book signing? Email Jesse at jesse@mrjesseross.com with your request.

Jesse is available for the following opportunities:

Speaking: Jesse travels around speaking to audiences of all sizes about the lessons highlighted in the book. Jesse can tailor his presentation to your specific audience and the desired outcomes of the event.

Workshops: Jesse is known for delivering fun, engaging, and highly interactive sessions for groups of all sizes.

Parent Engagement Sessions: Jesse takes the lessons from the books and applies them to parental groups of all sizes with parent-student audiences to create better relationships at home.

Customized Training Sessions: Jesse can deliver a ½ day or full day sessions tailored to your event or audience that will help them apply the lessons to their careers, with ample time for one-on-one discussion and facilitated peer learning.

For More Information Contact Jesse Ross:

Instagram & Twitter: @mrjross

LinkedIn: rossjesse

YouTube: jesseross03

Email: jesse@mrjesseross.com

Website: www.mrjesseross.com

Phone: 612-598-7236